MW01172269

DISCOVER YOUR JOY

DISCOVER YOUR JOY:
The Self-Care Journal

Krystal Meldrum

No part of this publication shall be reproduced, transmitted, or sold in whole or in part in any form, without the prior written consent of the author.

© Copyright 2019 Meldrum Studios. All rights reserved.

To my sisters, daughter, and sisters-in-law: Autumn, Rashelle, Jessica, Cherise, Chelsea, MaraLyn, Katie, Ashley, Melinda, Alina, Delany, and Alyssa. I hope each day you will take a little time for self-reflection, self-care, and self-love. I pray you will create numerous and regular experiences of joy, contentment, and surpassing happiness!

CONTENTS

HABITS OF HAPPY PEOPLE
that Anyone Can Learn

Many women today are stressed and overwhelmed with all the demands of life. This simple journal is a powerful tool. In only five minutes a day, it can help you reconnect with yourself, discover what brings you joy, and create daily moments of happiness.

In the twentieth century, psychologists began to study behavioral and mental disorders. Scientists and psychiatrists discovered medications and therapies that helped stabilize people to a normal mood level. However patients weren't necessarily happy, just stable. Positive psychology began as a new domain of psychology in 1998 when Martin Seligman chose it as the theme for his term as president of the American Psychological Association. Only one out of one hundred studies researched in the twentieth century was studying healthy and happy people. Thus, positive psychology was born. Researchers started studying what happy people do to find what the commonality was for them and whether those behaviors could be duplicated. Could patients improve from stable to joyful? The resounding answer was, yes!

The common practices that were found to be most beneficial were meditation, flow moments, savoring life, gratitude, journaling, kindness practices, making personal goals, belief in a higher power, and having a purpose. *Discover Your Joy: The Self-Care Journal* has several ways to implement many of these tools. If used regularly, you will create more joy in your daily life.

The pursuit of happiness sometimes feels like searching for the illusive fountain of youth. The reality is the fountain of youth is a myth, and happiness is not a final destination. Happiness is a daily practice. As women, our lives are often one of putting out fires, mundane work, and caregiving. Some days we may even feel we don't have a single moment to do one thing we want to do.

Nurturing yourself through self-care is a way of creating boundaries so you can keep on giving in your many roles. It's important to have boundaries to prevent burnout. I remember when my children were small I really needed to exercise to de-stress and manage my neck pain. I would exercise in my living room to a video with my toddlers in the room. The biggest toddler would wrap his little body around my legs like a monkey holding on to a banana tree screaming that he wanted to play with me right now! I thought, "Can't I have a moment to exercise? Am I a bad mom?" I then realized I had already fed and dressed him, and now I needed to give him a boundary. I pulled him off my leg and looked into his big, beautiful eyes. I said, "I need to exercise right now so you can either exercise by me or play in this room while I exercise, but I am not playing with you right now. I can play with you after I am done." As I consistently explained this to my children, they eventually understood and supported my self-care needs.

You can create self-care boundaries too, and this journal can help. You will be prompted to write about the following things:

1. What are you grateful for?
2. What would make today amazing?
3. Describe a positive moment you experienced today or yesterday.

The first prompt, "What are you grateful for?", helps you establish a foundation for happiness by focusing on what you are grateful for each day. I have a personal witness of what powerfully therapeutic tools gratitude and writing are. There was a ten year period in my life where I struggled with depression. In order to consciously attempt to cut through the gloom, I made a goal to record at least four sentences a day in my journal about something I was grateful for. Some days I was so tired and depressed I didn't want to do it, but I was determined to keep my promise to myself. After all, it was only four sentences and I felt it was making a difference. This habit helped open my mind to more and more positive things in my life. In moments of doubt I would read back over what I had written. I immediately found that every day there were multiple reasons to be grateful – and there were often tiny miracles as well!

Eventually I was healed from depression, but the greater blessing was my brain started to work on autopilot in grateful thought patterns. In this life we find what we are looking for. By programming my mind to look for the positives for which to be grateful, I discovered more and more reasons to be happy. It felt like I had an internal magnet for attracting happiness to myself.

The second prompt, "What would make today amazing?", is an exciting question. Asking yourself this question gets the wheels in your brain turning to discover the answer. The home I grew up in taught me everything would work out for me if I put work before play and put the needs of the family first. This was true for me as a child because there were so many chances for fun with friends, church, and school. There were also opportunities to develop talents and pursue interests. So, back then, I always had a lot of fun. But as a mom, I learned there are so many demands that the only way to make time for "play" was to schedule it. Asking yourself the aforementioned question helps to cut through all the confusion in your day, find the best answer, and then schedule some fun into your day.

I want you to learn you are in charge of your life and you can do fun things! You have time. Years ago, my dad and my seven uncles ran a newspaper business. They would have a daily business meeting while eating lunch at a local restaurant that was famous for their homemade pie. They always ordered a whole pie and ate it first while their lunch orders were being prepared. Ordering dessert first ensured they would have room to eat it!

I remember the first time I experienced this. My parents and I were on a vacation in Maine at a darling diner. My dad ordered banana cream pie before our meal. I couldn't believe what we were doing! It was the most delicious banana cream pie I had ever had. The whipped topping was two inches thick, the filling was divine and the crust was flaky perfection! If you "eat your dessert" by doing self-care first, the work will still get done.

When I discovered the question "What would make today amazing?", it changed my life. My answer was never earth shattering. It was usually something small, simple, and doable like getting outside for a twenty-minute walk, reading, sketching, or playing a game with one of my kids. I soon realized the only thing standing in the way of the "amazing" things I wanted to do was myself. I found if I just took twenty minutes away from the daily chaos of life, I could do something that made my day feel amazing. It will astonish you how little time it takes to make "the amazing" become a reality in your life.

The final journal prompt is "Describe a positive moment you experienced today or yesterday". This will help you reflect on what your happiest moment was in the day. Notice the word *describe*. If you write in detail, describing what you saw, heard, felt, tasted, or touched, you will give yourself a chance to re-experience the moment, adding more joy into your life.

After the five journaling pages there are three booster pages that will help you further reflect, learn about yourself, and discover your personal happiness recipe.

The booster pages will prompt you to write about the following things:

1. The first gratitude booster page is a reflection page where you will write about your happiest moment over the past five journal entries. This can triple your joy because you enjoyed it in the moment, you enjoyed it when you wrote about it the first time, and then you get to enjoy it again when you fill out the weekly reflection page! I love the saying "We need to remember the June roses in the Decembers of our lives." This reflection journaling will help you remember the best moments in your life!

2. The next page invites you to think about your favorite things. You will record five things you love such as your favorite music or food so you can get to know yourself better.

3. The last page is a self-discovery page intended to help you understand yourself better. As you follow the prompts, you may gain interesting insights about yourself and learn how to treat yourself better.

My hope is that as you write in this journal you will become a better friend to yourself. I hope you gain a better understanding of your unique needs, your personality, your favorite things, your dreams and goals, and discover what brings you joy in your daily life. You can make a little time for you. You can do it. You are worth it!

FIVE COMMON HAPPINESS PITFALLS

Happiness is all about discovering what brings you joy, creating a daily self-care practice, understanding your expectations, and being cheerfully flexible if your planned schedule needs to be adjusted. Five areas many people struggle with are unmet expectations, housework, self talk, their relationship with their body, and guilt.

Unmet Expectations

Recently, my sister remodeled her home. Around the same time, my friend built a new home. In both cases, the projects took longer and cost three times the expected amount. Both women had such a negative experience that afterwards they experienced a severe health crisis. Every construction project I have seen in my life has always been that way, taking at least double the estimated time and money. We recently had a construction project which happened to follow this typical construction pattern and luckily I didn't have a meltdown because I was preprogrammed mentally with what to expect.

Expectations often have to be adjusted during life. One of my friends told me that she did her best to raise her sons in a religious home, but they have not chosen to follow in her faithful footsteps. This devastated her. In order to be happy, she learned to release her expectations of her sons' choices while also never giving up hope! No one can take away her hope, so she just patiently loves on.

What expectations are causing you grief? Can you own your expectations and make your needs known? Do you have expectations that would be better to release?

Housework

Having a clean home can be an expectation that can wreak havoc on a woman's happiness level, especially if she has children at home. Sometimes a woman feels about herself however the inside of her home looks. This is terrible because a clean home can become a disaster zone in a nanosecond!

How clean your home is shouldn't determine your happiness level, but for many years, this was how I felt. If my home was clean, I would let myself be happy. If it was dirty, I felt frustrated and tried to get everyone in my family to help me clean. I have some advice: if your children are young, do the best you can. Cleaning with three toddlers is what I call cleaning in a three-baby blizzard. That was the hardest time I ever had trying to keep up with my home. It's like trying to shovel snow when it's a blizzard outside. It doesn't seem like you are making a dent – but really you are. Just keep teaching them. They will eventually get older and you will be so happy you trained them when they were young! It's worth it.

Now I have older children and cleaning is so awesome! I taught my children how to work when they were small and they have self-esteem, focus, and skills. If you need more help with creating simple habits and systems to have a clean and orderly home so you can have more free time, check out my book *The Organize Your Joy Workbook: The Mom's Complete Organizing Guide*. Three of my favorite simple tips are: one, clean the kitchen after every meal, especially after dinner; two, don't put it down, put it away; and three, have your children do at least two chores a day that serve the family (cleaning their bedroom and doing their homework is not enough.) You want to train your children to not just serve themselves and be finishers, but to serve others and become extra milers.

Everyday my children do a job before and after school to clean the house. It is good that they are trained workers who understand what is expected, but one day it just made me feel sad when I realized that everyday they would come home from school and say, "Hey what are my jobs?" Which, interpreted, means, "Hey you, what are my jobs so I can get the heck out of here to go play with friends A.S.A.P.?" I wanted to connect with them and to hear about their day! So I got deliberate and invited them to play a game with me, go on a short walk right after school, or I would help them finish their jobs. My children were not very talkative, but when we played, walked, or worked together they would open up and talk about what was going on in their lives. My suggestion is to try to connect with your children each day through work or play or both.

I remember talking to my auto mechanic and he mentioned that his seventy-year-old mother regretted how important she had made cleaning the house be in her life over the years. It was paramount to her to have beauty and order! But now she regrets it because there were things she missed doing with her children because cleaning her home always took precedence. Keep this story in mind as you try to balance your time and energy.

Here's a fun way to connect with your home. When you are alone and the home is quiet, place your hand on one of the inner walls of your home. Then ask your home, "What is your name?" Listen for an answer. Then ask your home, "What do you need?"

When I asked my last home its name, she said, "Emerald." I then asked her what she needed. She said emotionally, "Please clean me!" So I tried to do better and clean more.

I have since moved. When I asked my new home it's name, he said, "Paul." When I asked what he needed, he said, "More laughter." Because of that, I've tried to be more lighthearted and fun.

This little exercise helps me feel connected with my home and helps me focus on what it and my family need most at any specific time.

Self Talk

In the next twenty-four hours, who will you be talking to more than any other person? Yourself, of course! Wherever you go, your Inner Narrator is there too. What does your Narrator sound like? Is the voice kind, apathetic, or harsh? Would you talk to a friend like that? Train your Inner Narrator to speak to you with kindness. What positive things can you say to yourself when your Inner Narrator starts being negative?

As long as you don't have unrealistic expectations and you are kind to yourself, you can become a good friend to yourself. People have a tendency to say to themselves I'll be happy when I am skinnier, richer, in a relationship, etc. Is that kind? Is that how you talk to your friends? What are some phrases that you tell yourself?

Phrases such as the following:
I'll be happy when ...
I'd be happy if ...
When _____ happens, then I'll be happy.

How can you flip negative phrases into positive ones? Instead of "I don't have time for self-care", you could say, "I can take five minutes a day for self-care." Instead of "I'll be happy when I lose weight", you could say, "I can get dressed up and look beautiful".

If you struggle with automatic negative thought patterns go to Byron Katie's website www.thework.com and do the exercises she suggests to become a positive thinker.

Your Relationship with Your Body

Many people use self-talk to criticize their appearance. Instead, fall in love with your body. Give yourself a five-minute oil massage or shower and thank each body part as you wash yourself. Start with your head, then your arms, hands, chest, buttocks, legs, and feet. Think thoughts of gratitude for the amazing creation that is your body. Your beauty is not a competition, you are a beautiful creation, perfect right now.

Consider starting a Positive Self-Talk Diet as your next weight loss program. Don't guilt yourself into any massive changes. Just start noticing if you say anything negative to yourself in your mind about your physical appearance. Write those words down. Whether it's true or not, replace it with a positive truth you want to believe. Write down your new replacement beliefs that you will say to yourself.

Either accept yourself or accept that you're going to change. There was a woman who had struggled with her weight her whole life, but she wanted to change. She decided to try the Positive Self-Talk Diet. She wondered if her struggle was not so much what she ate, but possibly more about what she thought of herself. She decided to try an experiment and not do any hard-core dieting but just get in control of her mind. Each day she told herself:

I am beautiful and perfect right now.
I am slender.
I am healthy and energized.
I love myself!

Her body transformed and she became her ideal shape and size. She ate from the garden, drank plenty of water, did moderate exercise, and got adequate sleep but her main focus was not lifestyle, but on training her brain in the language of positive self talk.

Guilt: Just Say No

One last bit of advice I want to add is that women in general experience a lot of guilt. My mom always said, "Don't do guilt." If you feel guilty about self-care than it's like filling a bucket with a hole in the bottom. The bucket can't fill up.

Self-care is important, so don't feel guilty taking time to meet your needs. It helps your soul and it shows children that being an adult can be fun and fulfilling, not just a life of performing duty upon duty. If kids view adulthood as miserable, they'll want to turn into adult Peter Pans who live in Neverland (a.k.a. your basement) and never grow up. Allow children to see how wonderful it is to be an adult by regularly practicing and modeling happiness and self-care.

AVOID THIS COMMON END-OF-LIFE REGRET

Everyone is interested in the pursuit of happiness, however, life is always changing so the mystical chalice of joy may seem illusive. Bronnie Ware, a woman who worked for years with the dying, wrote an article sharing "The Top Five Regrets of the Dying". One of the five regrets that people had was the following:

"I wish I had let myself be happier."

Bronnie explained in her TEDx Talk that we need to realize that although we all are going to die, we all have the gift of time right now. We can choose a life of haphazard distractions or a life of joy, meaning, and abundance.

You do not have to abandon your family or become selfish to do a little self-care each day. You will come to find that when you take time for self-care, not only will you be happier, you will actually have more to give!

So, how can you avoid the common regret of wishing you'd let yourself be happier? The first step is awareness. The second is to cultivate habits that help you experience daily happiness and the wonders of life. This journal is designed to help you build happiness skills in a short period of time so you can become happier, naturally.

LIFE IS A
Balancing Act

As women we have so many things we need to do or should do. It can seem like we are always "putting out fires" and not doing things we want to do. Sometimes we tell ourselves, "When my children go to school" or "When the kids move out" or "When I quit my job" then I will have time for me.

The truth is that you must learn to make time for yourself in every season of your life. It's a balancing act. Think of a scale with you on one side of the balance and everyone else on the other. You need to balance the concepts of self-care and caring for others.

In my experience and that of many moms I've talked to, sleep is a big issue. My mom took naps to keep her going and I'm grateful that I followed her example. Anytime I feel down or drained, a nap is usually all I need to feel better. As you consider self-care, please evaluate your sleep patterns and see if you need to improve them. Getting good sleep can make all the difference in the world for your attitude and energy.

Another thing I personally have needed to balance is getting time for my art. For fifteen years I could only grab fifteen minutes to an hour a day to write or sketch. This filled my bucket and made me feel happiness and satisfaction because something I did, stayed done. Now my children are older and I can paint for long stretches at a time. I struggle putting my paints down and putting my "mom hat" back on. I struggle wanting to clean, do laundry, and make dinner.

We have a family council meeting each week on Sundays. During one of these my twelve-year-old son gave me a good suggestion. He said on Saturdays and in the summer when the children are home that I could work or play with my team until lunchtime. Then they can go play after lunch and I can paint. What a great idea! I took his advice, and although it takes self-discipline, things have been working much better.

I often ponder a quote I once heard by Neal A. Maxwell where he said we can be "so busy checking on our own temperatures, we do not notice the burning fevers of others" around us. I tend to be a self-absorbed person that is often thinking of my needs. I try to quiet down my self-care needs, but not bury them. I tell my art self, "Calm down. I will paint sometime soon, but right now I am spending time with my children. I am going to enjoy this time with them because they are not always here, and my paints are always here."

The good news is that as women we are wired to be able to do good at a lot of things! We can connect to ourselves, our husband, our children, our family, God, others, and do a good job at all of them. Yes, there is a limit to what one person can do. And if you are dropping too many balls, then take a step back and look at your life to see if you feel balanced or not. Meditate or talk with a friend for extra help becoming self-aware.

I like to pray each morning. At the end of my prayer I ask God who should I serve that day. Then I just quietly listen. Sometimes a name floats into my mind, but some days, nothing floats in. On those days, I know that I am really empty, and I need to do a little extra self-care that day.

Life is always changing so you will need to evaluate your life all along the way and remember that you are meant to find happiness and satisfaction in every season.

HOW TO USE THE
Discover Your Joy Journal

1. Dedicate five minutes a day for journaling. This book makes it simple. Just fill in the blanks. The prompts help one reflect on gratitude and self-care. The likelihood of a great idea becoming a reality is greatly enhanced if it's written down.

2. Be consistent writing at the same time and in the same place each day. Make time to fill out the journal daily. This practice creates consistency while developing habits of focusing on the positives in your life. When and where would you like to write for five minutes? What works for your schedule: morning, afternoon, or evening?

3. Make your daily goals small and doable. I have found that the activities I choose are usually free. I love art, especially sketching. Sketching has helped me reignite my painting passion. I love to watch the paint dance on the canvas! I've included a few paintings on the next two pages to inspire you. The first one is called "She Is Growing" and the second is called "Nourish the Seed". When you make time for small self-care activities, it makes each day feel like a masterpiece!

"She Is Growing"

4. Strive to nurture yourself with self-care moments daily. If that's not practical at this point, try for at least 2-3 self-care moments each week. Do the best you can, so you can stay in touch with yourself, your needs, and happiness level.

"Nourish the Seed"

5. Create a Master Top 100 Self-Care List. As you journey through *Discover Your Joy: The Self-Care Journal*, you will think of your own self-care ideas and prompts. Don't just think about them, write them down on the space provided in the next section.

CREATING YOUR
Self-Care Master List

On the following pages, create your master list of 100 self-care ideas that you enjoy or think you may. After you do each activity, rate how much you enjoyed it with 1-5 stars for future reference. This list is a lifesaver, because when you need a boost, you have a list of ideas that you know you enjoy. Usually, when people are down, they have a tendency to blank out on ideas and think they don't have any time or energy, so they just go to the fridge or veg on electronics or go shopping. Do something you REALLY enjoy! You have the time. You just need to make a decision and be deliberate about it, even if it's just a fifteen-minute activity like walking in nature, journaling, or learning something new.

My mom always taught me to be my own best doctor, so when I go to the doctor I already know what is wrong with me and probably even how to fix it. Most of the time all I need is for my doctor to fill out an official prescription. Likewise, you can be your own best happiness doctor. Start figuring out what feeds your mind, body, and soul, so when you need a boost you can fill a happiness prescription from your self-care master list.

To get your think tank going, here are some things that might make your days amazing. Check any that interest you.

- ○ Call a friend.
- ○ Color.
- ○ Cook something.
- ○ Declutter.
- ○ Do deep, yoga-style breathing for 3+ minutes.
- ○ Do some EFT tapping. (See Brad Yates on YouTube.)
- ○ Do speed gratitude. As quickly as you can, think of things you're grateful for that start with every letter of the alphabet.
- ○ Do three things on my to-do list.
- ○ Do yoga for 15-20 minutes or try "laughter yoga" (on YouTube).
- ○ Draw.
- ○ Drop in at a thrift store.
- ○ Exercise.
- ○ Experience a sunrise or sunset.
- ○ Garden.
- ○ Go on a picnic.
- ○ Go to an aquazumba class.
- ○ Go outside and look at something in nature up close for 30 seconds. (Think Georgia O'Keeffe close.)
- ○ Go to bed early.
- ○ Go to the gym.
- ○ Have a dance party!
- ○ Laugh.
- ○ Learn on YouTube for 20 minutes.
- ○ Look at cloud formations. (See CloudAppreciationSociety.org.)
- ○ Look up new, fun recipes.
- ○ Make a vision board.
- ○ Meditate for 15 minutes. (Check out Jason Brotherson on YouTube.)

- Organize something small like a drawer or cabinet.
- Paint your nails.
- Participate in a support group with family or friends in person, online, or through an app like Marco Polo.
- Plan and do a family activity.
- Plan something to look forward to.
- Play in your garden, visit a greenhouse, or make a fairy garden.
- Practice, play, or learn to play an instrument.
- Read for 20 minutes.
- Read fun, clean jokes.
- Read to a child.
- Scrapbook with a child for an hour.
- Send a thank you note.
- Serve someone.
- Sing.
- Sketch.
- Spend 20 minutes in nature.
- Take a bubble bath or blow bubbles.
- Take a nap.
- Talk to an uplifting friend who is good at self-care and ask them what they do to take care of themselves.
- Visit a friend.
- Visit a library or bookstore.
- Walk outside 20 minutes.
- Watch a funny YouTube video.
- Watch anything by Nick Vujicic, an inspirational speaker born without arms and legs.
- Watch Olympic gold medal performances on YouTube.
- Work on a puzzle.
- Write for an hour; write a book or story, write in your journal, or just write your feelings out.

MY SELFCARE MASTER LIST

MY SELF CARE MASTER LIST
Give Each Activity 1-5 Stars

1. _____
2. _____
3. _____
4. _____
5. _____
6. _____
7. _____
8. _____
9. _____
10. _____
11. _____
12. _____
13. _____
14. _____
15. _____
16. _____
17. _____
18. _____
19. _____
20. _____

MY SELFCARE MASTER LIST

Give Each Activity 1-5 Stars

21. _____
22. _____
23. _____
24. _____
25. _____
26. _____
27. _____
28. _____
29. _____
30. _____
31. _____
32. _____
33. _____
34. _____
35. _____
36. _____
37. _____
38. _____
39. _____
40. _____
41. _____
42. _____
43. _____
44. _____
45. _____
46. _____

47. _____
48. _____
49. _____
50. _____
51. _____
52. _____
53. _____
54. _____
55. _____
56. _____
57. _____
58. _____
59. _____
60. _____
61. _____
62. _____
63. _____
64. _____
65. _____
66. _____
67. _____
68. _____
69. _____
70. _____
71. _____
72. _____
73. _____

MY SELF CARE MASTER LIST

74. _____
75. _____
76. _____
77. _____
78. _____
79. _____
80. _____
81. _____
82. _____
83. _____
84. _____
85. _____
86. _____
87. _____
88. _____
89. _____
90. _____
91. _____
92. _____
93. _____
94. _____
95. _____
96. _____
97. _____
98. _____
99. _____
100. _____

DISCOVER YOUR JOY

Journal Pages

Date:

What am I grateful for today?

1. _____

2. _____

3. _____

What would make today amazing?

1. _____

2. _____

3. _____

Describe a positive moment you experienced today or yesterday.

_____

_____

_____

_____

_____

_____

_____

Date:

What am I grateful for today?

1. _____
2. _____
3. _____

What would make today amazing?

1. _____
2. _____
3. _____

Describe a positive moment you experienced today or yesterday.

_____
_____
_____
_____
_____
_____
_____
_____

Date:

What am I grateful for today?

1. _____

2. _____

3. _____

What would make today amazing?

1. _____

2. _____

3. _____

Describe a positive moment you experienced today or yesterday.

_____

_____

_____

_____

_____

_____

_____

_____

Date:

What am I grateful for today?

1. _____

2. _____

3. _____

What would make today amazing?

1. _____

2. _____

3. _____

Describe a positive moment you experienced today or yesterday.

_____

_____

_____

_____

_____

_____

_____

Date:

What am I grateful for today?

1. _____
2. _____
3. _____

What would make today amazing?

1. _____
2. _____
3. _____

Describe a positive moment you experienced today or yesterday.

_____

_____

_____

_____

_____

_____

_____

_____

REFLECTION PAGE

Review the past week and think about one experience you're especially grateful for. Write about it or draw something that will help you remember how wonderful it was.

GRATITUDE BOOSTER

"Food is for eating, and good food is to be enjoyed...
I think food is, actually, very beautiful in itself."
— *Delia Smith*

What are your favorite foods?

1. _____

2. _____

3. _____

4. _____

5. _____

Describe or draw one of your favorite foods.

SELF-DISCOVERY BOOSTER

Imagine yourself as a baby. If desired, put a photo of yourself as a baby on this page and on your mirror. Project your love to this beautiful little child. Write positive, encouraging words to yourself on this page. What do you say to yourself when you look in the mirror? Would you say unkind things to this baby like it's ugly or overweight? Of course not! Say something to the picture on the mirror such as, "You are adorable!" Say it until you believe it.

Date:

What am I grateful for today?

1. _____
2. _____
3. _____

What would make today amazing?

1. _____
2. _____
3. _____

Describe a positive moment you experienced today or yesterday.

_____
_____
_____
_____
_____
_____
_____
_____

Date:

What am I grateful for today?

1. _____

2. _____

3. _____

What would make today amazing?

1. _____

2. _____

3. _____

Describe a positive moment you experienced today or yesterday.

_____

_____

_____

_____

_____

_____

_____

_____

Date:

What am I grateful for today?

1. _____
2. _____
3. _____

What would make today amazing?

1. _____
2. _____
3. _____

Describe a positive moment you experienced today or yesterday.

_____
_____
_____
_____
_____
_____
_____

Date:

What am I grateful for today?

1. _____

2. _____

3. _____

What would make today amazing?

1. _____

2. _____

3. _____

Describe a positive moment you experienced today or yesterday.

_____

_____

_____

_____

_____

_____

_____

_____

Date:

What am I grateful for today?

1. _____
2. _____
3. _____

What would make today amazing?

1. _____
2. _____
3. _____

Describe a positive moment you experienced today or yesterday.

_____
_____
_____
_____
_____
_____
_____
_____

REFLECTION PAGE

Review the past week and think about one experience you're especially grateful for. Write about it or draw something that will help you remember how wonderful it was.

GRATITUDE BOOSTER

"If the simple things of nature have a message that you understand, rejoice, for your soul is alive."

— *Eleonora Duse*

What are your favorite places in nature?

1. _____

2. _____

3. _____

4. _____

5. _____

Describe or draw one of your favorite places in nature.

SELF-DISCOVERY BOOSTER

If you could go on any vacation and everything was all taken care of where would you go and why? What does this tell you about what you are wanting and needing right now?

Date:

What am I grateful for today?

1. _____

2. _____

3. _____

What would make today amazing?

1. _____

2. _____

3. _____

Describe a positive moment you experienced today or yesterday.

_____

_____

_____

_____

_____

_____

_____

_____

Date:

What am I grateful for today?

1. _____
2. _____
3. _____

What would make today amazing?

1. _____
2. _____
3. _____

Describe a positive moment you experienced today or yesterday.

_____
_____
_____
_____
_____
_____
_____

Date:

What am I grateful for today?

1. _____
2. _____
3. _____

What would make today amazing?

1. _____
2. _____
3. _____

Describe a positive moment you experienced today or yesterday.

_____
_____
_____
_____
_____
_____
_____
_____

Date:

What am I grateful for today?

1. _____
2. _____
3. _____

What would make today amazing?

1. _____
2. _____
3. _____

Describe a positive moment you experienced today or yesterday.

_____
_____
_____
_____
_____
_____
_____

Date:

What am I grateful for today?

1. _____

2. _____

3. _____

What would make today amazing?

1. _____

2. _____

3. _____

Describe a positive moment you experienced today or yesterday.

_____

_____

_____

_____

_____

_____

_____

REFLECTION PAGE

Review the past week and think about one experience you're especially grateful for. Write about it or draw something that will help you remember how wonderful it was.

GRATITUDE BOOSTER

"To me there is no picture so beautiful as smiling, bright-eyed, happy children; no music so sweet as their clear and ringing laughter."

— *P.T. Barnum*

What are your favorite sounds?

1. _____

2. _____

3. _____

4. _____

5. _____

Describe or draw one of your favorite sounds or draw something that makes that sound.

SELF-DISCOVERY BOOSTER

Record in detail what a joyful day would look like to you. Not a holiday, just imagine a normal, wonderful day in your own home. What are the sights, sounds, smells, and feelings you would experience?

Date:

What am I grateful for today?

1. _____

2. _____

3. _____

What would make today amazing?

1. _____

2. _____

3. _____

Describe a positive moment you experienced today or yesterday.

_____

_____

_____

_____

_____

_____

_____

_____

Date:

What am I grateful for today?

1. _____
2. _____
3. _____

What would make today amazing?

1. _____
2. _____
3. _____

Describe a positive moment you experienced today or yesterday.

_____
_____
_____
_____
_____
_____
_____

Date:

What am I grateful for today?

1. _____
2. _____
3. _____

What would make today amazing?

1. _____
2. _____
3. _____

Describe a positive moment you experienced today or yesterday.

_____

_____

_____

_____

_____

_____

_____

_____

Date:

What am I grateful for today?

1. _____

2. _____

3. _____

What would make today amazing?

1. _____

2. _____

3. _____

Describe a positive moment you experienced today or yesterday.

_____

_____

_____

_____

_____

_____

_____

_____

Date:

What am I grateful for today?

1. _____
2. _____
3. _____

What would make today amazing?

1. _____
2. _____
3. _____

Describe a positive moment you experienced today or yesterday.

_____
_____
_____
_____
_____
_____
_____
_____

REFLECTION PAGE

Review the past week and think about one experience you're especially grateful for. Write about it or draw something that will help you remember how wonderful it was.

GRATITUDE BOOSTER

"Nothing can beat the smell of dew and flowers and the odor that comes out of the earth when the sun goes down."
— *Ethel Waters*

What smells do you love?

1. _____

2. _____

3. _____

4. _____

5. _____

Describe or draw something that smells good to you.

SELF-DISCOVERY BOOSTER

In what ways do you like to pamper yourself? Do you like to pick or buy fragrant flowers, get your nails done, soak in a bubble bath, or take a nap? If you don't feel like you can pamper yourself, why not?

Date:

What am I grateful for today?

1. _____
2. _____
3. _____

What would make today amazing?

1. _____
2. _____
3. _____

Describe a positive moment you experienced today or yesterday.

_____
_____
_____
_____
_____
_____
_____
_____

Date:

What am I grateful for today?

1. _____

2. _____

3. _____

What would make today amazing?

1. _____

2. _____

3. _____

Describe a positive moment you experienced today or yesterday.

_____

_____

_____

_____

_____

_____

_____

_____

Date:

What am I grateful for today?

1. _____
2. _____
3. _____

What would make today amazing?

1. _____
2. _____
3. _____

Describe a positive moment you experienced today or yesterday.

_____

_____

_____

_____

_____

_____

_____

Date:

What am I grateful for today?

1. _____

2. _____

3. _____

What would make today amazing?

1. _____

2. _____

3. _____

Describe a positive moment you experienced today or yesterday.

_____

_____

_____

_____

_____

_____

_____

_____

Date:

What am I grateful for today?

1. _____

2. _____

3. _____

What would make today amazing?

1. _____

2. _____

3. _____

Describe a positive moment you experienced today or yesterday.

_____

_____

_____

_____

_____

_____

_____

_____

REFLECTION PAGE

Review the past week and think about one experience you're especially grateful for. Write about it or draw something that will help you remember how wonderful it was.

GRATITUDE BOOSTER

"Let the rain kiss you. Let the rain beat upon your head with silver liquid drops. Let the rain sing you a lullaby."
— *Langston Hughes*

What are your favorite things to feel?

1. _____

2. _____

3. _____

4. _____

5. _____

Describe or draw one of your favorite things to feel.

SELF-DISCOVERY BOOSTER

What are your favorite parts of your body and why?

Date:

What am I grateful for today?

1. _____

2. _____

3. _____

What would make today amazing?

1. _____

2. _____

3. _____

Describe a positive moment you experienced today or yesterday.

_____

_____

_____

_____

_____

_____

_____

_____

Date:

What am I grateful for today?

1. _____
2. _____
3. _____

What would make today amazing?

1. _____
2. _____
3. _____

Describe a positive moment you experienced today or yesterday.

_____

_____

_____

_____

_____

_____

_____

_____

Date:

What am I grateful for today?

1. _____

2. _____

3. _____

What would make today amazing?

1. _____

2. _____

3. _____

Describe a positive moment you experienced today or yesterday.

_____

_____

_____

_____

_____

_____

_____

_____

Date:

What am I grateful for today?

1. _____
2. _____
3. _____

What would make today amazing?

1. _____
2. _____
3. _____

Describe a positive moment you experienced today or yesterday.

_____
_____
_____
_____
_____
_____
_____
_____

Date:

What am I grateful for today?

1. _____
2. _____
3. _____

What would make today amazing?

1. _____
2. _____
3. _____

Describe a positive moment you experienced today or yesterday.

_____
_____
_____
_____
_____
_____
_____

REFLECTION PAGE

Review the past week and think about one experience you're especially grateful for. Write about it or draw something that will help you remember how wonderful it was.

GRATITUDE BOOSTER

"Never, ever underestimate the importance of having fun."
— Randy Pausch

What emotions do you enjoy the most?

1. _____

2. _____

3. _____

4. _____

5. _____

Describe or draw something that reminds you of
one of your favorite emotions.

SELF-DISCOVERY BOOSTER

Imagine you get to meet your very most optimal self. This is the highest and happiest version of yourself. What would she be like?

Date:

What am I grateful for today?

1. _____
2. _____
3. _____

What would make today amazing?

1. _____
2. _____
3. _____

Describe a positive moment you experienced today or yesterday.

_____

_____

_____

_____

_____

_____

_____

_____

Date:

What am I grateful for today?

1. _____

2. _____

3. _____

What would make today amazing?

1. _____

2. _____

3. _____

Describe a positive moment you experienced today or yesterday.

_____

_____

_____

_____

_____

_____

_____

Date:

What am I grateful for today?

1. _____

2. _____

3. _____

What would make today amazing?

1. _____

2. _____

3. _____

Describe a positive moment you experienced today or yesterday.

_____

_____

_____

_____

_____

_____

_____

_____

Date:

What am I grateful for today?

1. _____

2. _____

3. _____

What would make today amazing?

1. _____

2. _____

3. _____

Describe a positive moment you experienced today or yesterday.

_____

_____

_____

_____

_____

_____

_____

_____

Date:

What am I grateful for today?

1. _____
2. _____
3. _____

What would make today amazing?

1. _____
2. _____
3. _____

Describe a positive moment you experienced today or yesterday.

_____
_____
_____
_____
_____
_____
_____
_____

REFLECTION PAGE

Review the past week and think about one experience you're especially grateful for. Write about it or draw something that will help you remember how wonderful it was.

GRATITUDE BOOSTER

"Books may well be the only true magic."
— *Alice Hoffman*

What are your favorite books?

1. _____

2. _____

3. _____

4. _____

5. _____

Describe or draw one of your favorite books. What is special about it? Why is it among your favorites?

SELF-DISCOVERY BOOSTER

What are you enjoying learning right now? Is there anything you would like to learn in this season of your life? (If you feel like you don't have time to learn what you want to learn, watch Josh Kaufman's TEDx Talk "The first 20 hours — how to learn anything" for ideas.)

Date:

What am I grateful for today?

1. _____
2. _____
3. _____

What would make today amazing?

1. _____
2. _____
3. _____

Describe a positive moment you experienced today or yesterday.

_____
_____
_____
_____
_____
_____
_____
_____

Date:

What am I grateful for today?

1. _____
2. _____
3. _____

What would make today amazing?

1. _____
2. _____
3. _____

Describe a positive moment you experienced today or yesterday.

_____
_____
_____
_____
_____
_____
_____
_____

Date:

What am I grateful for today?

1. _____

2. _____

3. _____

What would make today amazing?

1. _____

2. _____

3. _____

Describe a positive moment you experienced today or yesterday.

_____

_____

_____

_____

_____

_____

_____

Date:

What am I grateful for today?

1. _____
2. _____
3. _____

What would make today amazing?

1. _____
2. _____
3. _____

Describe a positive moment you experienced today or yesterday.

_____

_____

_____

_____

_____

_____

_____

_____

Date:

What am I grateful for today?

1. _____
2. _____
3. _____

What would make today amazing?

1. _____
2. _____
3. _____

Describe a positive moment you experienced today or yesterday.

_____
_____
_____
_____
_____
_____
_____

REFLECTION PAGE

Review the past week and think about one experience you're especially grateful for. Write about it or draw something that will help you remember how wonderful it was.

GRATITUDE BOOSTER

"Colors are the smiles of nature."
— *Leigh Hunt*

What are your favorite colors and why?

1. _____

2. _____

3. _____

4. _____

5. _____

Draw or color something that is your favorite color, or describe one of your favorite colors and why you like it.

SELF-DISCOVERY BOOSTER

If you could wear anything you wanted without any negative
repercussions, what would you wear and why?

Date:

What am I grateful for today?

1. _____

2. _____

3. _____

What would make today amazing?

1. _____

2. _____

3. _____

Describe a positive moment you experienced today or yesterday.

_____

_____

_____

_____

_____

_____

_____

_____

Date:

What am I grateful for today?

1. _____
2. _____
3. _____

What would make today amazing?

1. _____
2. _____
3. _____

Describe a positive moment you experienced today or yesterday.

_____

_____

_____

_____

_____

_____

_____

Date:

What am I grateful for today?

1. _____
2. _____
3. _____

What would make today amazing?

1. _____
2. _____
3. _____

Describe a positive moment you experienced today or yesterday.

_____

_____

_____

_____

_____

_____

_____

Date:

What am I grateful for today?

1. _____
2. _____
3. _____

What would make today amazing?

1. _____
2. _____
3. _____

Describe a positive moment you experienced today or yesterday.

_____

_____

_____

_____

_____

_____

_____

_____

Date:

What am I grateful for today?

1. _____

2. _____

3. _____

What would make today amazing?

1. _____

2. _____

3. _____

Describe a positive moment you experienced today or yesterday.

_____

_____

_____

_____

_____

_____

_____

REFLECTION PAGE

Review the past week and think about one experience you're especially grateful for. Write about it or draw something that will help you remember how wonderful it was.

GRATITUDE BOOSTER

"Any glimpse into the life of an animal quickens our own and makes it so much the larger and better in every way."
— *John Muir*

What are your favorite animals and why?

1. _____

2. _____

3. _____

4. _____

5. _____

Describe or draw one of your favorite animals.

SELF-DISCOVERY BOOSTER

If you could be any animal, what would it be and why? What do these
things tell you about yourself and what you need right now?

Date:

What am I grateful for today?

1. _____
2. _____
3. _____

What would make today amazing?

1. _____
2. _____
3. _____

Describe a positive moment you experienced today or yesterday.

_____

_____

_____

_____

_____

_____

_____

Date:

What am I grateful for today?

1. _____
2. _____
3. _____

What would make today amazing?

1. _____
2. _____
3. _____

Describe a positive moment you experienced today or yesterday.

_____

_____

_____

_____

_____

_____

_____

Date:

What am I grateful for today?

1. _____
2. _____
3. _____

What would make today amazing?

1. _____
2. _____
3. _____

Describe a positive moment you experienced today or yesterday.

_____
_____
_____
_____
_____
_____
_____

Date:

What am I grateful for today?

1. _____
2. _____
3. _____

What would make today amazing?

1. _____
2. _____
3. _____

Describe a positive moment you experienced today or yesterday.

_____
_____
_____
_____
_____
_____
_____
_____

Date:

What am I grateful for today?

1. _____
2. _____
3. _____

What would make today amazing?

1. _____
2. _____
3. _____

Describe a positive moment you experienced today or yesterday.

_____
_____
_____
_____
_____
_____
_____
_____

REFLECTION PAGE

Review the past week and think about one experience you're especially grateful for. Write about it or draw something that will help you remember how wonderful it was.

GRATITUDE BOOSTER

"Dance like no one is watching. Sing like no one is listening. Love like you've never been hurt. And live like it's heaven on Earth."

— *Mark Twain*

What are your favorite sports or kinds of dance to watch or do? (Also, make a note of any you would like to try!)

1. _____

2. _____

3. _____

4. _____

5. _____

Describe or draw one of your
favorite sports or kinds of dance.

SELF-DISCOVERY BOOSTER

How do you feel about time, especially as it relates to things you *want* to do? Could you benefit from writing a new belief about time?

Date:

What am I grateful for today?

1. _____
2. _____
3. _____

What would make today amazing?

1. _____
2. _____
3. _____

Describe a positive moment you experienced today or yesterday.

_____

_____

_____

_____

_____

_____

_____

Date:

What am I grateful for today?

1. _____
2. _____
3. _____

What would make today amazing?

1. _____
2. _____
3. _____

Describe a positive moment you experienced today or yesterday.

_____

_____

_____

_____

_____

_____

_____

Date:

What am I grateful for today?

1. _____
2. _____
3. _____

What would make today amazing?

1. _____
2. _____
3. _____

Describe a positive moment you experienced today or yesterday.

_____

_____

_____

_____

_____

_____

_____

Date:

What am I grateful for today?

1. _____
2. _____
3. _____

What would make today amazing?

1. _____
2. _____
3. _____

Describe a positive moment you experienced today or yesterday.

_____

_____

_____

_____

_____

_____

_____

_____

Date:

What am I grateful for today?

1. _____

2. _____

3. _____

What would make today amazing?

1. _____

2. _____

3. _____

Describe a positive moment you experienced today or yesterday.

_____

_____

_____

_____

_____

_____

_____

_____

REFLECTION PAGE

Review the past week and think about one experience you're especially grateful for. Write about it or draw something that will help you remember how wonderful it was.

GRATITUDE BOOSTER

"A table, a chair, a bowl of fruit, and a violin; what else does a man need to be happy?"

— *Albert Einstein*

What are five possessions you love having in your life?

1. _____

2. _____

3. _____

4. _____

5. _____

Describe or draw one of your favorite possessions.

SELF-DISCOVERY BOOSTER

We live in a world full of stuff. How do you feel about your possessions? Do they support you in doing things that bring you joy? Would you feel energized if you spent some time decluttering, organizing, and creating space for things you want to do? What small thing could you do to create space for something you love?

Date:

What am I grateful for today?

1. _____

2. _____

3. _____

What would make today amazing?

1. _____

2. _____

3. _____

Describe a positive moment you experienced today or yesterday.

_____

_____

_____

_____

_____

_____

_____

_____

Date:

What am I grateful for today?

1. _____

2. _____

3. _____

What would make today amazing?

1. _____

2. _____

3. _____

Describe a positive moment you experienced today or yesterday.

_____

_____

_____

_____

_____

_____

_____

Date:

What am I grateful for today?

1. _____

2. _____

3. _____

What would make today amazing?

1. _____

2. _____

3. _____

Describe a positive moment you experienced today or yesterday.

_____

_____

_____

_____

_____

_____

_____

_____

Date:

What am I grateful for today?

1. _____
2. _____
3. _____

What would make today amazing?

1. _____
2. _____
3. _____

Describe a positive moment you experienced today or yesterday.

_____

_____

_____

_____

_____

_____

_____

Date:

What am I grateful for today?

1. _____

2. _____

3. _____

What would make today amazing?

1. _____

2. _____

3. _____

Describe a positive moment you experienced today or yesterday.

_____

_____

_____

_____

_____

_____

_____

_____

REFLECTION PAGE

Review the past week and think about one experience you're especially grateful for. Write about it or draw something that will help you remember how wonderful it was.

GRATITUDE BOOSTER

"Today is life - the only life you are sure of. Make the most of today. Get interested in something. Shake yourself awake. Develop a hobby. Let the winds of enthusiasm sweep through you. Live today with gusto."

— *Dale Carnegie*

What are your favorite hobbies?
(Also, note any hobby ideas you'd like to try!)

1. _____
2. _____
3. _____
4. _____
5. _____

Describe or draw one of your favorite hobbies.

SELF-DISCOVERY BOOSTER

Fast forward to the last years of your life. Imagine you are sitting on a porch in a rocking chair watching the sunset. You think over the past and feel complete contentment, peace, and joy. What are things (relationships, hobbies, accomplishments) that you experienced over your lifetime to create such satisfaction and happiness?

Date:

What am I grateful for today?

1. _____

2. _____

3. _____

What would make today amazing?

1. _____

2. _____

3. _____

Describe a positive moment you experienced today or yesterday.

_____

_____

_____

_____

_____

_____

_____

Date:

What am I grateful for today?

1. _____
2. _____
3. _____

What would make today amazing?

1. _____
2. _____
3. _____

Describe a positive moment you experienced today or yesterday.

_____
_____
_____
_____
_____
_____
_____
_____

Date:

What am I grateful for today?

1. _____

2. _____

3. _____

What would make today amazing?

1. _____

2. _____

3. _____

Describe a positive moment you experienced today or yesterday.

_____

_____

_____

_____

_____

_____

_____

Date:

What am I grateful for today?

1. _____
2. _____
3. _____

What would make today amazing?

1. _____
2. _____
3. _____

Describe a positive moment you experienced today or yesterday.

_____

_____

_____

_____

_____

_____

_____

Date:

What am I grateful for today?

1. _____

2. _____

3. _____

What would make today amazing?

1. _____

2. _____

3. _____

Describe a positive moment you experienced today or yesterday.

_____

_____

_____

_____

_____

_____

_____

REFLECTION PAGE

Review the past week and think about one experience you're especially grateful for. Write about it or draw something that will help you remember how wonderful it was.

GRATITUDE BOOSTER

"Friends... they cherish one another's hopes. They are kind to one another's dreams."

— Henry David Thoreau

Who are five favorite friends?

1. _____

2. _____

3. _____

4. _____

5. _____

Describe or draw something you love about your friends.

SELF-DISCOVERY BOOSTER

What are some things you enjoy doing with your friends? What things would you like to do with them in the future?

CLOSING
Thoughts

Dear friend,

I am so happy this journal came into your life! I hope you have learned a lot about yourself and have learned to integrate self-care habits into your weekly routine.

I want to remind you that no matter how hard life is, there is always something to be grateful for. We just have to look for it. Even if it's sunshine, air to breathe, or five minutes of solitude.

I love the following idea:

"It's not happiness that brings us gratitude,
it's gratitude that brings us happiness."

How true! I hope you will continue to find things to be grateful for, and that you will create joyful experiences all your life.

Your friend,

Krystal Meldrum

ACKNOWLEDGMENTS

To Mom and Dad, thank you for your perseverance and your wise teachings that help me create such a happy and abundant life.

I appreciate my husband for giving me freedom and generous resources to pursue my dreams and goals.

Thanks to my children for being so helpful, hardworking, and understanding so I could accomplish one of my goals by publishing this book. I hope each of you will pursue a passion too!

I want to thank my dear friend Tina Albrecht for her incredible enthusiasm, organizing abilities, and editing skills. You always understand my vision and are always concerned about helping others find the best tools to create more joy in their lives.

Also, thank you Lindsay Elworthy for making the message of the book so fresh and clear with your fabulous cover and graphic design.

Finally, I love my Heavenly Father for being there for me through good times and bad and for giving me so many opportunities.

ABOUT
the Author

Krystal Meldrum graduated from Brigham Young University with a Bachelor's of Fine Art in Illustration in 2001. Krystal enjoys painting, writing, organizing, and teaching. She also loves country dancing, traveling, reading, and aquazumba. Her voice as an artist has been described as a color dancer that captures themes of strengthening marriages and families. She and her husband, Jeremy Meldrum, reside in Salem, Utah and are the parents of six energetic children. She is the author of *The Organize Your Joy Workbook: The Mom's Complete Organizing Guide.*

Krystal is passionate about her new series of picture books which will help parents teach their children about joy, character, and organizing.

Follow Krystal's Organizing Journey at www.OrganizeYourJoy.com and on Instagram @OrganizeYourJoy.

Follow Krystal the Color Dancer's art at:
Instagram: @krystalmeldrum
Facebook: @krystalmeldrumthecolordancer
Website: https://krystalmeldrum.com
YouTube: https://krystalmeldrum.com/youtube

Made in the USA
Columbia, SC
14 October 2022

69270679R00090